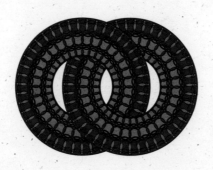

THE
LAUNDRESS
CATCHES
HER BREATH

Paola Corso

THE
LAUNDRESS
CATCHES
HER BREATH

CavanKerry ◈ Press LTD.

CavanKerry Press Ltd.
Fort Lee, New Jersey
www.cavankerrypress.org

Library of Congress Cataloging-in-Publication Data

Corso, Paola.
The laundress catches her breath / by Paola Corso. -- 1st ed.
p. cm.
ISBN 978-1-933880-31-0 (alk. paper)
ISBN 1-933880-31-7 (alk. paper)
I. Title.

PS3603.O778L38 2012
813'.6--dc23

2012006496

Cover photograph by Walker Evans, U.S. Library of Congress
Cover and interior text design by Gregory Smith
First Edition 2012, Printed in the United States of America

CavanKerry Press is proud to publish the works
of established poets of merit and distinction.

CavanKerry Press is grateful for the support it receives
from the New Jersey State Council on the Arts.

Other Books by Paola Corso

POETRY

Once I Was Told the Air Was Not for Breathing (2012)

Death by Renaissance (2004)

A Proper Burial (2003)

PROSE

Catina's Haircut: A Novel in Stories (2010)

The Politics of Water: A Confluence of Women's Voices
Coedited with Dr. Nandita Ghosh (2007)

Giovanna's 86 Circles and Other Stories (2007, 2005)

per la mia cugina

Another world is not only possible, she is on her way.
On a quiet day, I can hear her breathing.

Arundhati Roy

CONTENTS

III. And Exhale

THE
LAUNDRESS
CATCHES
HER BREATH

I. Inhale

Bias

She washes colors but prefers whites,
    bleaching streaks of yellow and mottled gray

grease on her apron from a shift at the fryer, stains
that can't hide in dyes of mulberry or hunter green.

She takes them on
    face to face like school girls she fought
                            and snapped in two.

She walks away with a loose tooth that she yanks out,
    tarred from cigarette smoke. She couldn't
get it white no matter how hard

                    she scrubbed.

Step by Step with the Laundress

1. It's easier to wash clean clothes if wearing clean clothes,
a saying adapted from your college-educated uncle who says it's
easier to find a job if you have a job when he hears you chewed
out Stubby for cutting back your hours at Eat'n Park.

2. Sort clothes in neat piles on the basement floor beside the safe
where your father Mister Twenty Horns stashes company photos
from mill picnics and prayer cards for every deceased member
of the family, alphabetized by saint.

3. Check pockets for matches, lighters, cigarettes left from break,
a string of beads Unc bought for job interviews but you wore
to bar bingo and stuffed in a pocket because it felt like bugs
around your neck.

4. Load the washer, set the dial, and pour in double the detergent,
knowing old man Twenty Horns waters it down since you told him
to either stop buying the cheap-ass Giant Eagle brand or you'd quit
doing his laundry.

5. As soon as the clothes are submerged in soapy water, have a
cigarette and listen to Tom Jones until the line "Whoa, whoa,
whoa, she's a lady" or your butt burns out. Whichever comes first.

6. When the load begins to agitate, drink your coffee on the porch
beside your grandmother's scrub board and hand wringer that
Twenty Horns will make you use if his water bill gets any higher
from trying to get mill soot out of his work clothes and the soup
of the day off yours.

7. Hang a taut line. Keep a clothespin in your mouth as if
smoking a cigarette while your work friend Donna finishes
your hoagie because her daughter ate hers and you gave yours
up for adoption.

8. Group clothes and hang together except don't put your
36 D hooter holders next to Donna's 32 AAA because you
know who will figure out you've been washing her clothes
since she got fired and kick your ass all the way to a laundromat.

9. Have a cigarette on the porch while the clothes dry. Then check
on your dying uncle next door as soon as your father stops yelling
about you getting another pay cut at Eat'n Park, so you'll never get
the hell out of his house.

10. Get rid of the wasp nest near the line because Twenty Horns
is too cheap to hire an exterminator and says you'll blow them away
with your smoker's cough. Tell him smoking like a chimney
ain't as bad as him smoking what a stack at the mill belches out so
he'll get the cancer, not you.

11. Take clothes down from the line, then see if you can go offer
to change your uncle's pillowcase next door because it's moist
from his shallow breath and you suddenly need him to see you
wearing the beads he gave you, if he remembers why.

12. Fold the clothes. Out of respect for your uncle, plan to wear
a clean uniform from the basket if you need to visit the funeral home
someday soon, then go straight to work at Eat'n Park rather than call
in sick. You want to believe what he told you.

Cigarettes and Coffee

Wish the hell he'd take a vacation, so I wouldn't have to wash his work clothes on my day off. I got my own uniforms to clean—waffle batter, soup mix, grease from the fryers. Good thing is Twenty Horn's clothes are so smoky I can have my cigarette while doing his load. I can spill my coffee on 'em and it don't matter. They're so sooty I don't waste my bleach—the gray they get is lighter than black, and come the next day, black is always darker than gray.

Now when is he gonna learn to empty his pockets out? It figures, no cash. This Juicy Fruit is goin' straight into the trash. I should wash his union card and see if his name comes off. I'd write mine in, find me work that pays like his. Unc wants better for me, something along the lines of a female position. J. C. Penney's would be nice. Montgomery Ward is across the river.

But I could do my old man's job. I got muscle. I could beat the crap outta a lump of coal or a beam of steel. Whatever he does. I smoke three packs a day so nothing that goes up his nose is news to me. I'll put it on my application papers. Make me qualified. Buy me a house bigger than his.

The Laundress Catches Her Breath

She swore off cigarettes, thinking
the cost of the cartons she'd save
every week would be enough

money to rent a room, move
out of her father's house.
But then Stubby cut her hours

again and the Maytag suds
saver broke the same day.
She was right in the middle

of a rinse when gray recycled water
flooded the garage floor. She kicked
the machine square in the gut,

didn't care what her father said
about conserving water, didn't care that
they had had that machine for as long as

she's been driving—her aunt
was right to use clean water
and not a suds saver. They stopped

making them in 2001, which
told her something. She kicked
it again and rescued her clothes out

of the filthy water. Before she could
mop the floor, her father came back
from church, drove his four-door

sedan halfway into the garage.
He saw a dirty river run toward
his new whitewall tires, slammed

the brakes, got out, grabbed
her clothes, and threw them
on the ground to soak up

the water. The sight sent her
out the door for a smoke, though
she told her dad she was going

to call a repairman. She ran
to her car parked up the street,
got in and rolled up the windows

so she could inhale through
her mouth and nose as if sitting
in the chambers of her lungs.

Coal Fire Smoke

1
Nothing left but her ashes,

the yard a pit of cigarette butts,
she crosses over to say a few words
to her neighbor's widowed dad,

a lump of tan man visiting from Georgia.
"You're good lookin', Mr. Slater—
that much I can see, love bug."

And under the surface of khaki
        a lump of wallet that
        burns and burns steady.

2
"Please, call me Wally."

She offers to keep house
for him, iron his boxer
shorts with creases

heat up beef potpies
in the oven until peas
flame on the fork.

Wallie puts his hand on her shoulder
        and smiles. "I'm old enough
        to be your father."

3

Her dad charges over,

mouth wide open, his breath
spiraling in her face. He's ready to yell
at her but doesn't when Wally says,

"Sounds like your daughter must be
good to have around the house."
She doesn't want to hear his answer,

leaves to put out her butt,
        one long cylinder of ash
        ready to flake and fall.

Colors in White

atrium

He sits

up in bed, looks out

the window, wondering if
        he'll set foot on the sidewalk
again, step onto the porch, stand on
                the welcome mat.
                        Even in his slippers.

cameo

Before work

she makes an appearance

brief so the smell of cigarettes and grease
        on her uniform won't turn
his stomach. She offers to wash
                the pillowcase.
                        He's too tired to lift his head.

antique

She remembers

how he filled out her first

job application after her father said,
        See your uncle. He went

to college, not me. She places
            a clean handkerchief
                        in her uncle's hand and leaves.

                decorator's
                       Later

        that evening he lets go of the handkerchief.

After a double shift, she washes,
        starches and presses
it, ready for presentation
           like a folded napkin
                on the table.

              dove
                   She imagines

      opening it, feathers

dropping slowly
        to the ground. He sees
white rising, rising
          whiter, distancing
              the sky.

Hole

The laundress picks up a shovel and digs. She tries
not to think about missing her uncle's funeral 'cause Stubby

changed her work schedule at the last minute and told her
to come in early to fill in for Marla May who called in sick

at the last minute when she woke up in bed with a tickle
in her throat and Stubby woke up with a tickle in his cock

beside her. She digs a hole one foot deep, wants to forget how
she smoked three packs and burnt the chicken nuggets.

She kept them in oil so she could picture Stubby's balls breaded
and browned to a crisp, knowing some old lady with no teeth

was gonna complain. She digs a hole two feet deep, hoping
her father doesn't come home early and find out what she's

about to bury in his yard. She digs a hole three feet deep
and knows what he'd say if he noticed a fresh mound of dirt

she'd say she weeded to plant flowers. She digs a hole four
feet deep. Since when did she give a damn about flowers

when she yanked every blooming thing in sight so she wouldn't
have to smell something sweet instead of her cigarette smoke?

She digs a hole five feet deep and remembers when she bought
her mother a corsage for her silver wedding anniversary party

because she deserved to smell something besides all his shit for once
in 25 years. She digs a hole six feet deep, puts down her shovel,

wraps a blanket around Donna's puppy, puts a garbage bag over it,
sets it in the grave. Donna lives in an apartment and didn't know

what to do with it. The laundress doesn't know what she's going
to do with the white carnation she bought to lay on her uncle's coffin.

She smells the flower, then tosses it down the hole. She buries
the blackness with her last shovel of dirt and still sees white.

II. Hold for Ten Seconds

One Thousand One

She opens her father's suitcase and empties it into the washing machine: a quilt the color of yellowed teeth, buttons and bugs sewn on, its patches smelling of lake sorrowed by stream, threads crusted on cotton weave. So heavy with his past, the quilt drops to the bottom, so heavy with his past the Maytag sinks into the ground. She reaches for a ladder and climbs down.

One Thousand Two

She reaches for a ladder and climbs down. The washing machine lid pops up. A wooden mother appears holding a baby with a black bird on its shoulder.

The laundress jumps back, screaming, "What the!" She pauses and sees that the statue doesn't move, so she charges forward. "Dirty as hell. Leave it to my old man to bring this home from his deer-huntin' cabin and expect me to work a miracle with bleach. And he calls himself a Catholic. Piss on it."

When the laundress reaches to throw the figure out with lint from the dryer, mother draws near and says, "Kiss me. Your lips won't turn black."

One Thousand Three

Mother draws near and says, "Kiss me. Your lips won't turn black."

The laundress spits. "A dirty mouth to go with your dirty body. We don't talk like 'at round here, lady. And in front of a baby. Na-ah. Open wide and let me clean it out with a little soap." She grabs the statue, throws it back into the washer, and slams the lid shut.

A voice echoes out. "*Nera sum sed formosa*. I am black but beautiful."

When there's silence, the laundress opens the lid a crack and peeks in. The mother pecks the laundress on the bridge of her nose.

One Thousand Four

The mother pecks the laundress on the bridge of her nose. She runs to a mirror to look for a black mark, but her skin is lighter. The mother smiles and says, "The blacker I am, the whiter you become."

"Yunz are black alright," the laundress agrees as she tips a bottle of bleach over the mother's head.

The mother replies, "The whiter I become, the blacker you are."

The laundress stops pouring.

One Thousand Five

The laundress stops pouring. "For your information, love bug—and I can call you that 'cause you laid a smooch on me—I ain't never gonna be black, but I can make you white. Trust me. I ain't afraid of no stain."

"You already are," the mother answers.

"Already what?"

The mother takes a step toward the laundress. "Black. Sicilian black."

The laundress steps back. "No way am I black!"

"Where do you think your father got me?"

The laundress snickers before she answers, "In a Vatican half-price reject pile on one of his trips to It-lee."

The mother shakes her head. "Your father's grandmother in Sicily kept me under her pillow, and so does he."

One Thousand Six

"Your father's grandmother in Sicily kept me under her pillow, and so does he."

The laundress lights a cigarette, keeping it between her lips as she speaks. "So that makes him a saint and me a sinner." Her nostrils close and open with each drag. "Now my uncle. He was a saint, so he was. But you don't know much about my old man, do you? Why do you think I want to get the hell outta here. That damn Stubby keeps cutting back my hours."

The mother motions for the laundress to exhale in another direction. "Please," she insists, "The baby."

The laundress shrugs and says as the smoke streams out of her nostrils, "He's Jesus. He'll live."

One Thousand Seven

"He's Jesus. He'll live. That much I know from the nuns. Besides, I'd take cancer over the cross any day."

"Put that cigarette out or I'll do it for you," the mother demands. "I've had enough smoke with votive candles lit at my feet all day."

When the laundress hesitates, the mother grabs it and puts it out on her own chest without flinching. The laundress gasps. "And stop thinking about getting my skin clean. It's not black from soot and smoke like your filthy lungs. My skin is dark because I'm the Black Madonna from Tindari."

One Thousand Eight

"My skin is dark because I'm the Black Madonna from Tindari. I'm black because light is matter and darkness is pure Spirit. *Nera. Scura. Bruna.* I'm black because I have the power to heal. Each and every year, thousands of pilgrims humble themselves before my image. They come with their braces and crutches and beg me to cure them. They leave behind their *tavolette* offerings of thanks, pieces of cloth with words and drawings of how I healed their children who fell out of windows, men trampled by horses, people sick in bed, soldiers injured in war, how I helped them after deadly earthquakes, volcanic eruptions, waves of plague. They come to me in their moment of danger."

"Then where were you when my uncle died? He had a tumor in his lungs the size of a steel mill and never worked in one. Why him and not my father? And he quit the smokes a long time ago. Why him and not me? I couldn't even wash his pillowcase for him because he was too weak to lift his head. The one thing I coulda done. So I washed it clean. After he died."

The laundress removes a neatly folded square of cotton tucked in her bra and speaks through tears. "I washed away his last breath."

One Thousand Nine

"I washed away his last breath." The laundress drops her head and weeps. "At night, I kept his pillowcase with me. Before I went to bed, I ran my finger around the stain from his oxygen hose. The smell of his breath put me to sleep. It's gone."

The Black Madonna nods. "Once a woman traveled from afar to thank me for saving her little girl's life. When she climbed the bluff to the chapel after a long journey, she couldn't believe my face was black. The moment she recoiled, her little girl, who had wandered off, fell from a cliff. The woman begged me to save her child's life. But the miracle had been done. The sea withdrew, so the girl could fall on sand. The woman now believed in the powers, and the sea kept its distance as a reminder. That was her miracle. And this is yours."

One Thousand Ten

"That was her miracle. And this is yours." The Black Madonna leans down to kiss the pillowcase and hands it to the laundress with the breath stain back on it. "The circle of darkness is pure Spirit. It will never disappear no matter how many times you wash this."

The laundress inhales the scent of her uncle and smiles. "You brought him back!" She hugs the Madonna so hard, the black bird flies off the Child's shoulder. The laundress backs away, dropping the pillowcase. "Did my uncle send you? He was the only one who could help me 'cause he was the only one I listened to. He even gave me some beads to wear for job interviews and I'd wear 'em if I ever got one, but that ain't gonna happen. He wasted his breath on me."

The bird lands on the pillowcase, but the laundress doesn't shoo it away. The Madonna motions for the bird to return to the Child's shoulder and for the laundress to pick up the pillowcase. The Madonna holds it to her cheek. "Listen for his breath. Just listen."

When the laundress hears her uncle's whisper, she makes it her own. She breathes in. She breathes in.

III. And Exhale

The Laundress

I

Sheets are wet

worrisome mounds
        in the basket, socks
            a pair of sorry balls

        dripping in self-pity,

underwear a limp limbo
        of cotton blends
            no longer soaking wet

        and not yet dry

waiting to be hung by a woman
        who scrubs away
            original sin

        on a rock

along the stream
        with her hands
            and the strength

        of resolve.

2

Sheets are hung

on the line, socks
        clipped at the heel,
                drawers droop

        with fear

of never taking shape
        from human proportion,
                a clothesline low in the middle

        as if bowing its head, waiting

    to be propped up by a woman
            who raises this offering
                    that much closer

        to where

the air gathers
        puffs of wind
                with breath enough

        for divine intention.

Blow Out the Candles

there was
        no twister
        out her window
no gale

spinning
              a black cloud

she mused
        at the shingled pyramid
        floating above her
she dreamt

        her father climbed
          a ladder

and tried to yank
             the roof down

her uncle attempted
        to use reason
        how long
could it defy

        gravity
           how long

before she pictured
           a baby

in her arms
    each hiccup
    lifting the roof
lowering it

    until she put the child
        on her breast

and the roof grew
        still

but she missed
    the sky
    she missed
its blue mission

    the clouds that pillowed
        her thoughts

and elevated them
        to dream

she blew out
    her baby's candle
    and as the pyramid
drifted off

    she knew it was
        her own breath

reaching for
        the possibility of air

Heiress to Air

In one nostril

steam, in the other

stink
fumes
smoke

as she steps over to the fryers at work

when sleepy little Marla May

accidentally pours something

other than batter into the waffle iron

and it ignites

like a furnace of steel.

The laundress falls to the ground

coughing, apron over her nose

as she crawls outside to the parking lot and collapses,

remembering

a tailpipe
a yellow line
a fire whistle.

When she wakes up

the air
flashes
crystal

and she follows it before it shatters

into pieces

all the way to a neon sign for a bar

on again
off again
twin tubes

inside the scent of margarita and menthol,

people with face masks

bright eyes

glowing in light.

Confused, she asks for

a beer
bar bingo
dark paneling

someone with a hangover or headache

but the bartender says what she needs

is a boost

a 15-minute session, a dollar a minute

to sniff
out the if
and when

to oxidize her day.

He tells her his name is O

his skin is breezy
his hair windblown
his eyes all circles & currents.

The laundress puts up her dukes.

"Honey," he says, "Leave those fists

at the door. You're in

a five-star oxygen bar."

She frowns, tries to bum a cigarette

before getting back to the Belgian waffles.

He says inhaling smoke

is like swallowing a chicken bone. She'll choke

to death.

"Sure you don't want to try a hit of O

do something for those

jet-lagged eyes
that hazy hair &
mucked-up disposition

perhaps an oxygen facial to plump out your skin with our special blend of

aerial
aerobic
aerosolic air?"

"Out your ass," she coughs.

She's used to breathing the smokestack

on her father's work clothes.

Her lungs could take a mill job.

He puts it to her this way: she can

breathe in heaven or hell.

Just look in the mirror:

red eyes
white skin
blue lips

She could have been patriotic

for the first time in her life

if she waved a flag at him

instead of her middle finger.

O takes a deep breath

puffs out his chest

and shows her the door.

This time no fist, she can't resist.

She grabs his mask, puts it to her crotch, spreads her legs and says,

> "Hang me
> out to dry.
> I'm yours, baby."

"Oh, so you want to live longer."
"Na-ah."

"Then you want to die happy."
"Yeah."

She bats her lashes and grunts for O

and she doesn't mean Oxygen.

He sits her down in a reclining chair

leans her head on a fluffy pillow

gives her a cloud to hold

He winks, tells her it's on the house.

He inserts twin tubes into her nostrils

      a double blow
      from on high
      cutting through

            the sails, the wings, the harp singing.

                Her first instinct

    is to reach for a particle coursing through the sky

          but she can't catch it.

Then her arms go limp where the clearing ends

             and the color begins.

        There is space
between her thoughts
between her toes
a breath of air

          from O. He'll show her

what she couldn't see before

be a mill hunk like Old Man Twenty Horns

more money more smoke more laundry

if she wants it. He'll show her union jobs

up and down the river valley

steel works, mirror works, a shot with your beer works

coal works
coke works
smoke in your lung works

scrap works zinc works down another drink works

rubber works iron works plate glass crew

He'll show her work conditions, air emissions

weather conditions and more:

nitrogen oxide
with a twist of dioxide
and carbon monoxide

all ready to roll.

O begins at her father's mill, and when Twenty Horns—

nuggets of coal for eyes, steel beams for legs

arms the length of a smokestack—

sees his daughter, he fires a tank of oxygen

a silver bullet whizzing toward her with the hose attached

to a nose.

She ducks and bolts, but Twenty Horns lassos her with the hose

and hurls her back to his coke works in the river town of Clairton

    a battery* of ovens
    16 tons of coal
    16 hours of heat

        charging, coking, pushing

laborers with their shovels, jam cutters their blades

    larry men in larry cars*

      top oven workers with wooden shoes,

    respirators and a pack of filters

with 16 times more lung cancer

      if she wants it.

*A battery is a number of coke ovens lined up in a row
*Larry operators "push" the coke out of the oven into cooling and transport cars

"Go on, take my job," Twenty Horns dares his daughter.

"I'll take it."

"You'd take it for an hour and quit!"

"I'll take it, and give me that stack, too,

I'll smoke it!" she dares him back.

The laundress tugs at the hose to free herself

but Twenty Horns hog-ties her. "How about my house?

Are you gonna take that too? Blow off the roof
                    with that cough
                    of yours!"

He flings her back to O to show her more.

No sense talking. Says her head is as hard as a 2 by 4.

O unties the laundress and points the nose down the river.

It follows an odor

coming from the mill in the town of Donora,

the grime on cars
with headlights
in the afternoon

a job with overtime

a factory worker taking a shower

a woman washing clothes. By the time she pins

the last of the load on the line

the first hung is dirty again.

O asks the laundress how about it

more money more smoke more laundry

if she wants it.

Before she can answer, everyone is covered

in a blanket of cold air over Mon Valley,

smoke

from the zinc works rises six feet then stops

cold.

Blackness

filling streets and homes, workers stumbling to the gate

drivers steer by scraping the curb

traffic comes to a halt

a football in the haze but no players can be seen on the field

the sound of a referee's whistle, a voice from the loudspeaker

instructs the crowd: Home.
                                             Go home.
                                             Go home now.

The laundress begs O to take her far away from her father,

                                   not home, so he points the nose north.

It takes a deep breath and exhales them to a river town along the Ohio

          that threatens
          to pick itself up
          and move upwind

          away from the filth of the aluminum smelter at Neville Island

from the benzene and acrylonitrile

       found in air samples

              taken by those Bucket Brigade people

                                    she's seen on TV.

One talked in a microphone about how the valley's coal-smudged skies

      once ran like spigot water

           from chimneys and stacks.

     Nurses changed their masks every five minutes

            they become so black.

        Show cows fattened
        and fussed over
        keeled over at the county fair

with their tongues hanging out and nobody

        with a clean hand to wave to the beauty queen.

  "She's only queen for a day. Let's go,"

            the laundress chokes.

The nose sneezes them to Keystone Lake,

      ice is thinner
      than the lipstick
      on her cigarettes,

                dirtier than

the nicotine on her teeth. She watches the fumes

    from car exhaust melt the ice before her eyes and when a fisherman

   reels in a trout and cuts it open

           he finds her cigarette lighter.

"So that's where I left it," the laundress hacks, reaching for it

      and a smoke in her pocket. When she can't stop

          wheezing

she says, "Keep the lighter. It's yours."

Then the laundress tosses the fisherman her pack of cigarettes.

"No. Use it to light a fire. It's friggin' freezing out here!"

Too cold to breathe, she says.

"You mean too polluted

to breathe. You're gasping for air," O scolds her.

He chips a black icicle forming out of the nose's nostril, puts it to her lips

tells her
take a lick
of this

"Hey, I gave him my cigarettes, didn't I? It was easier

popping my cherry than doin' that!"

She snaps the other icicle off the nose and points it another direction.

When it catches its breath,

the nose snorts them all the way back to her nonna

                as a garment worker

hunchbacked on a stool felling coats
                for 14 hours

    sitting so close to the others, she smells

their breath
on her face
feels the heat
                of their bodies

    hands too numb to know the prick

            of a needle, eyes so close to the coat

    she sees the fire in each stitch

The laundress gropes around, looking for a window to open

                but there is none.

She remembers how her grandmother told her

no factory in Pittsburgh

would produce gowns and delicate blouses

because the black smoke from the mills

would ruin them.

That's why they made

only goods
dark in color
coarse in material

coats and overalls and corduroy workshirts

Not like those Italian girls

in New York City, *cugine* at the shirtwaist factory

trapped   behind a locked factory door

so they couldn't leave with a fancy blouse in their pocketbook. O shows her

girls leaping from sewing table

to sewing table across the floor

choking in a smoky cloakroom

as their dresses catch fire

pushed to the ledge by flames,

crowding for air

windows popping
girls jumping
three and four together

"Give 'em some air!" the laundress cries,

dodging smoke. She grabs the nose,

puts it on a worker like a respirator.

"No use, she's dead," O tells her.

O pulls the laundress away, takes her to a Pittsburgh Pirates T-shirt factory

where an old Haitian woman slips on oily papers

that cover the floor

fractures her arm

and despite the pain

stays there
four hours
until the shift ends

because nobody is allowed to stop working to help.

The laundress finds a pay phone, calls an ambulance

but the floor supervisor hangs up the receiver. She'd kick him in the balls

if she had the strength to lift her leg.

"Know what they say in Pittsburgh?

No sweatshops, Bucco!"

The floor supervisor laughs at her
      so the laundress musters her strength.

                    She rips off her shirt

rolls it up into a baseball and hurls it into his gut.

                        He collapses and so does she.

      "That's it!
      I quit cigarettes.
      Quit cursing

                my old man. I don't want his factory job.

Don't want my dirty lungs.

      I promise I'll make 'em come clean if you stop," the laundress moans.

"Home," she pleads, gasping for air.
                    "Take me home now."

She and O and the nose start back,

                         and from high in the clouds
          they see a blast furnace

                         smoke rising

a factory on fire, a river

          two rivers, then three

             before the city's Golden Triangle is in flames.

Firefighters sift through rubble for gold bands in the gray ash.

Cops wake up one night

             with blood coming out of their eyes

                    glass lodged
                    in their lungs
                    from doing time

     at the Point.

As a plume of gas and fumes trail close behind the laundress,

the wind gods take pity on her, blow her

back to the parking lot, to the back seat of a co-worker's car

back home to her father's house,

back to her own bed where she lies feverish,

coughing

and out of breath. They call an ambulance.

A voice from India dispatches the call.

The paramedic lies on her body and blows

in her mouth
in her nostrils
in her navel.

When she doesn't respond, the paramedic asks her father

                    to inhale what could be her last breath.

       He says he's had enough

          of her second-hand smoke
          doesn't want her
          three packs a day

says she'll get well enough to keep him awake at night,

              cough herself to sleep.

       He asks the ambulance workers to get

a respiratory therapist to revive her

                 with an impulse of breath.

Next a doctor jabs her with a steroid

makes her smoke a pipe
of clean air, shows her
an X-ray of her lung

says she's a candidate for emphysema and has walking pneumonia.

Bed rest for a week.

When she gets home, she takes half a pill so they last longer

and plans to go to work the next day.

Those doctors
are rich but she
needs the money.

She doesn't have health insurance. And what if Twenty Horns does

his own laundry

and kicks her out of the house?

She gazes out her bedroom window,

sees a tank of oxygen

delivered
to her doorstep
like a bottle of milk

remembers her uncle reaching for his

and a tube connecting

his nose

to the life source

a ball and chain keeping him indoors

except for chemotherapy

She waves until he spots her.

                  He holds up his tank as if to say cheers

     then walks back inside

               before she asks him how to use it.

                She yells out for him

but he doesn't answer,

      doesn't see she reaches in her pocket for the beads

         he gave her to wear for an interview
                    at Penney's.

   As she whispers his name

     she sees a black bird rising from his chimney,

        a blast of smoke
        that engulfs his house
        and blazes in her eyes.

She doesn't move

doesn't breathe

when the bird swoops
down

covering her in fiery wings.

Scorched by the heat

the bird grows still, petrified in ashes.

Its wings fall like a flicked butt.

She breathes inside

its downy feathers
nera scura bruna
darkness of spirit

of home.

Air Patterns

She pins panties on the line between buxom clouds round with water weight. Her bra is beside two padded patches lifted by the breeze. A slip next to a thin layer of overcast.

Once it begins to rain,

the wind picks up

in circles and feathers.

The clothesline rises and falls, rises and falls with thunder. Pins hold on, clouds float up, undergarments fall. She runs with her basket to gather them from the grass and sees

a butterfly land on the eyes

of a child who wishes

to be awakened from sleep.

Coffee, No Cigarettes

The laundress cleans out the pockets
of her father's work pants. She's got

Twenty Horns down to ten now since
she's been wearing her beads to work.

He asks her in a regular voice to go easy
on softener. He likes his uniforms stiff, says

they don't stick to him as much in the heat.
She puts his union card and loose change

on the shelf with the detergent, fishes in
his pocket and pulls out a pack

of Juicy Fruit with a stick left. She rips
off the wrapper, holds it between her lips

like a cigarette. She chews until the flavor
fades, spits it out, sips her coffee.

A Well-Ventilated Basement Apartment

She flashes a charge card and her middle finger then leaves her father's house to move into her own apartment during a flash flood while her uncle puts on a pair of boots and shines a flashlight in the closet. There he finds a crate—inside it are some old pay stubs and a card she never gave him, the words written in the controlled cursive she hasn't used since Catholic school. She wades to an open window, takes a breath deep enough to air out her past, to exhale the ghost inside her.

ACKNOWLEDGMENTS

Thanks to the editors of *VIA:Voices in Italian Americana* for publishing some of these poems as first runnerup for the 2004 Bordighera Poetry Prize, to the prize's co-founders Daniela Gioseffi and Alfredo dePalchi, and to judge Donna Masini.

I would also like to thank the editors who published the following poems (sometimes under different titles):

Chance of a Ghost: An Anthology of Contemporary Ghost Poems (Helicon Nine Editions): "A Well-Ventilated Basement Apartment"

Days I Moved Through Ordinary Sounds: The Teachers of WritersCorps in Poetry and Prose (City Lights Books): "Step by Step with the Laundress," "The Laundress Catches Her Breath"

Italian Americana: "The Laundress"

Lavanderia: A Mixed Load of Women, Wash, and Word (City Works Press): "Bias"

MARGIN: Exploring Modern Magical Realism: "Blow Out the Candles," "Air Patterns," "Heiress to Air"

More Sweet Lemons: Writings with a Sicilian Accent (Legas) and *Sentence: A Journal of Prose Poetics*: "The Laundress Catches Her Breath in Ten Seconds"

Subtropics: "Step by Step with the Laundress"

Finally, I would like to acknowledge the following authors and their works, which I consulted when writing some of these poems:

Devra Davis, *The Secret History of the War on Cancer* (Basic Books, 2007).

_____, *When Smoke Ran Like Water* (Basic Books, 2003).

John Graham and David Holtgrave, "Coke Oven Emissions: A Case Study of Technology-Based Regulation," *1 Risk* 243 (1990): 244-47.

Don Hopey and David Templeton, "Mapping mortality: A Post-Gazette series that examines air pollution in Western Pennsylvania," *Pittsburgh Post-Gazette*, Dec. 12-19, 2010.

Carol K. Redmond et al., "Long-Term Mortality Experience of Steelworkers," *Journal of Occupational Medicine* 17, no. 1 (1975): 40-43.

Joseph Sciorra, "The Black Madonna of East Thirteenth Street," *New York Folklore Society Voices*, Vol 30. Spring-Summer 2004.

Leon Stein, *The Triangle Fire* (ILR Press, 2001).

David Von Drehle, *Triangle: A Fire That Changed America* (Grove Press, 2004).

CAVANKERRY'S MISSION

Through publishing and programming, CavanKerry Press connects communities of writers with communities of readers. We publish poetry that reaches from the page to include the reader, by the finest new and established contemporary writers. Our programming brings our books and our poets to people where they live, cultivating new audiences and nourishing established ones.

OTHER BOOKS IN THE NOTABLE VOICES SERIES

CavanKerry now uses only recycled paper in its book production. Printing this book on 30% PCW and FSC certified paper saved 2 trees, 1 million BTUs of energy, 127 lbs. of CO_2, 67 lbs. of solid waste, and 524 gallons of water.